Africa Is Not A Country ...

It's a Continent!

by
Arthur Lewin, Ph.D.
and
Africa Unlimited

To the memory of
Enoch DeCordova Bromfield
and
Eli Augustus Lewin, Sr.

Africa Unlimited

Cheryl Johnson, John Anderson

*Mary Avilez, Morduant Edwards,
Rolaine Frederique, Sophia Frayar, Athenia Henry,
Kenneth Jones, Patricia Jones, Albert Lockwood,
Andrew Morrison, Carline Murphy, Colin Roach,
Alic Scott, Dennis Sterling*

"Africa Knows No Boundaries!"

CLARENDON Publishing Company
Milltown, New Jersey

© Copyright 1996

ISBN 0-9628911-1-8

Africa Is Not A Country: It's A Continent!

Are we African?

How big is Africa?

What is apartheid?

How far away is Africa?

Can we return to Africa?

Can Mandela end apartheid?

How many people live in Africa?

Would the Africans welcome us?

How many countries are in Africa?

Which is the richest country in Africa?

Which is the biggest country in Africa?

Is Africa bigger than the United States?

How did slavery begin? How did it end?

Where in Africa did the slaves come from?

Is Africa rich or poor? Is she modern or backward?

Which US Congressman died for the people of Africa?

Why did South Africa let Nelson Mandela out of prison?

Africa Is Not A Country:
It's A Continent!

by

Dr. Arthur Lewin

Available at Black Bookstores
Everywhere

Africa Is Not A Country: It's A Continent!

CONTENTS

CHARTS

PUZZLES

PICTURES

▲ FUN FOR THE WHOLE FAMILY

▲ TEACHERS, USE IT IN YOUR CLASS

▲ TRY THE PUZZLES AND THE GAMES

▲ KIDS, YOU CAN COLOR THE PICTURES

▲ EVERYTHING YOU ALWAYS
WANTED TO KNOW ABOUT AFRICA

▲ TEST YOUR KNOWLEDGE OF THE
MOTHERLAND WITH YOUR FRIENDS

▲ PARENTS, READ IT TO YOUR
CHILDREN, OR HAVE YOUR KIDS
READ IT TO YOU

Africa Unlimited

The two principal organizers of Africa Unlimited are *Cheryl Johnson* and *John Anderson*. They spent many an afternoon in Harlem's Schomburg Center for Research in Black Culture diligently digging up data for our files. They also visited many embassies, bookstores and street fairs. They drew up detailed fact sheets for each African country. John, like Cheryl, is heavily involved with the Black Church. Cheryl reports that her family, and a knowledgeable Sunday school teacher, fed and developed her interest in her African roots.

Dennis Sterling is a senior majoring in accounting. His expertise is on the Central African country of Rwanda. For several years he has been an invaluable student aide to all the professors in the Black and Hispanic Studies Department. He greatly assisted me in this project and in all my endeavors.

Kenneth Jones helped us develop the puzzles and games. He earned a degree in management at Baruch College in 1988. *Mary Avilez* always brought her two wonderful children, Curtis and Joy, to our Saturday morning sessions. She is an expert on South Africa and Aids in Africa. *Colin Roach* graduated from Baruch in 1990, majoring in marketing and minoring in education. He wrote two poems for us, and was the campus poet. He says that the purpose of his writing is to "help Caribbean and African peoples all over the world understand themselves and the environment in which we live." He is expert on African liberation movements.

Alic Scott is a high school student from Albany, New York. He and his younger sister, Nikky, wrote us with many ideas for this book. They are truly a credit to their parents, Brenda and Tony Scott, who inspired them with a strong, vibrant African consciousness.

Carline Murphy majors in Finance and Investments at Baruch, and is an expert on Tunisia. She has used her computer skills to draw up the statistical profiles of the countries of Africa that will appear in the next edition. Her lively daughter, Milina, came every Saturday morning. On the way home together with Mary Avilez, and her two children, they would usually stop off at a bookstore to dig up a few more key facts about the Motherland.

Albert Lockwood has been interested in Black History ever since he was able to read. He works for a re-insurance agency in the Wall Street area during the day, and attends Baruch at night. He possesses extremely detailed knowledge of Zambia and its world-reknowned leader, Kenneth Kaunda. He also has an excellent grasp of the geography of the African continent.

Rolaine Frederique, Morduant Edwards, Sophia Fryar and *Patricia Jones* all worked very hard on the artwork and text for the articles on African food, family and children. They have gathered a lot of material on the African family that we will use in later publications. Sophia was another member of Africa Unlimited who always brought her children to our Saturday gatherings. *Athenia Henry*, whose specialty is the Cameroon, also always had her two children in tow. So we see that Africa Unlimited is about family. We worked with our families, as a family, to gain an understanding of the African family of nations.

These are the fine young people who make up Africa Unlimited. Together with their help, and yours, we hope to ignite widespread, grassroots interest in amassing and understanding the details of the history, cultures and peoples of Africa. Please write us. Feel free to address your questions specifically to one of our members. *We will personally answer all letters.*

I have been a professor of Black Studies at Baruch College for 12 years. The energy, intelligence, ingenuity and creativity of our students is truly unbelievable.

Why We Wrote this Book?

We know a lot about the countries of Europe and the states of the United States. But how much do we know about the 52 countries of Africa? How many of their capitals can we name? How many African leaders can we identify? It is hard to be proud of a place we do not know, especially when everything we hear about it is negative.

"When you control a man's thinking you do not have to worry about his actions. You do not have to tell him not to stand here or go yonder. He will find his 'proper place' and will stay in it. You do not need to send him to the back door. He will go without being told. In fact, if there is no back door, he will cut one for his special benefit. His education makes it necessary."

So wrote Carter G. Woodson in <u>The Mis-Education of the Negro</u> in 1933. He argued that even those of us with college degrees were ignorant of the history and culture of our people. He said that we were being trained to feel and act inferior. Is that still not true today? Are the schools teaching our children the history, culture and contributions of our people? Do the newspapers report our positive accomplishments? Does the media cast us in roles that we can truly be proud of?

We will not have a real future until we know that we have a real past. We will not rise until we know that we are a people with a land that thrives and grows. We will never attain equality in this "land of immigrants" until we know that we come from somewhere, from the land that is the mother of all mankind. Africa is our land, and it is not a country. It is a continent, the richest continent on the face of the earth.

There have been many books written about Africa, and a number of them have been done by people of African descent. Black professors write their books, graduate students their dissertations and college students their term papers, to show that they are "qualified", that they have mastered their studies. This is all well and good. However, what we also need, and need very badly, is a book about Africa that the common man can understand, that the child can understand.

We need a book on Africa that tells a story, a good thrilling story that is, nonetheless, filled with facts. Yes, we need the minute details of our history and culture that our scholars are providing, but we also need _Africa is Not a Country_ so that we can keep the larger picture in mind. As we wander through the forest of detail that is our intellectual investigation of our culture, we must always be aware of where we are on the road of knowledge, and why we embarked on this great journey of discovery. It is to that end that we dedicate this book. Here is everything you always wanted to know about Africa, but could not find explained in simple, direct, exciting terms.

The 53 Nations of Africa

Algeria	Madagascar
Angola	Malawi
Benin	Mali
Botswana	Mauritania
Burkina Faso	Mauritius
Burundi	Morocco
Cameroon	Mozambique
Cape Verde	Namibia
Central African Republic	Niger
Chad	Nigeria
Comoros	Rwanda
Congo	Sao Tome & Principe
Cote D'Ivoire	Senegal
Djibouti	Seychelles
Egypt	Sierra Leone
Equatorial Guinea	Somalia
Eritrea	South Africa
Ethiopia	Sudan
Gabon	Swaziland
Gambia	Tanzania
Ghana	Togo
Guinea	Tunisia
Guinea-Bissau	Uganda
Kenya	Zaire
Lesotho	Zambia
Liberia	Zimbabwe
Libya	

Africa Was Our Home...
Africa Was Our Home...
Africa Was Our Home...

A frica was our home

F ar across the seas.

R e-awakening our forgotten past

I s an almost impossible task.

C an we succeed if we try?

A frica, can we find you?

Can We Find You?...
Can We Find You?...
Can We Find You?...

Area

Sudan	967,000	Ivory Coast	125,000
Algeria	920,000	Burkina Faso	106,000
Zaire	906,000	Gabon	103,000
Libya	679,000	Guinea	95,000
Chad	495,800	Ghana	92,000
Niger	489,000	Uganda	91,000
Angola	481,400	Senegal	75,800
Mali	478,800	Tunisia	63,000
Ethiopia	471,800	Malawi	46,000
South Africa	471,000	Benin	43,000
Mauritania	398,000	Liberia	43,000
Egypt	387,000	Sierra Leone	28,000
Tanzania	365,000	Togo	22,000
Nigeria	357,000	Guinea-Bissau	14,000
Namibia	318,000	Lesotho	11,700
Mozambique	310,000	Equatorial Guinea	10,800
Zambia	291,000	Burundi	10,700
Somalia	246,000	Rwanda	10,200
Central African Repub	241,000	Djibouti	8,500
Botswana	232,000	Swaziland	6,700
Madagascar	227,000	The Gambia	4,300
Kenya	225,000	Cape Verde	1,600
Cameroon	184,000	The Comoros	900
Morocco	72,000	Mauritius	790
Zimbabwe	151,000	Sao Tome/ & Principe	400
Congo	132,000	Seychelles	170

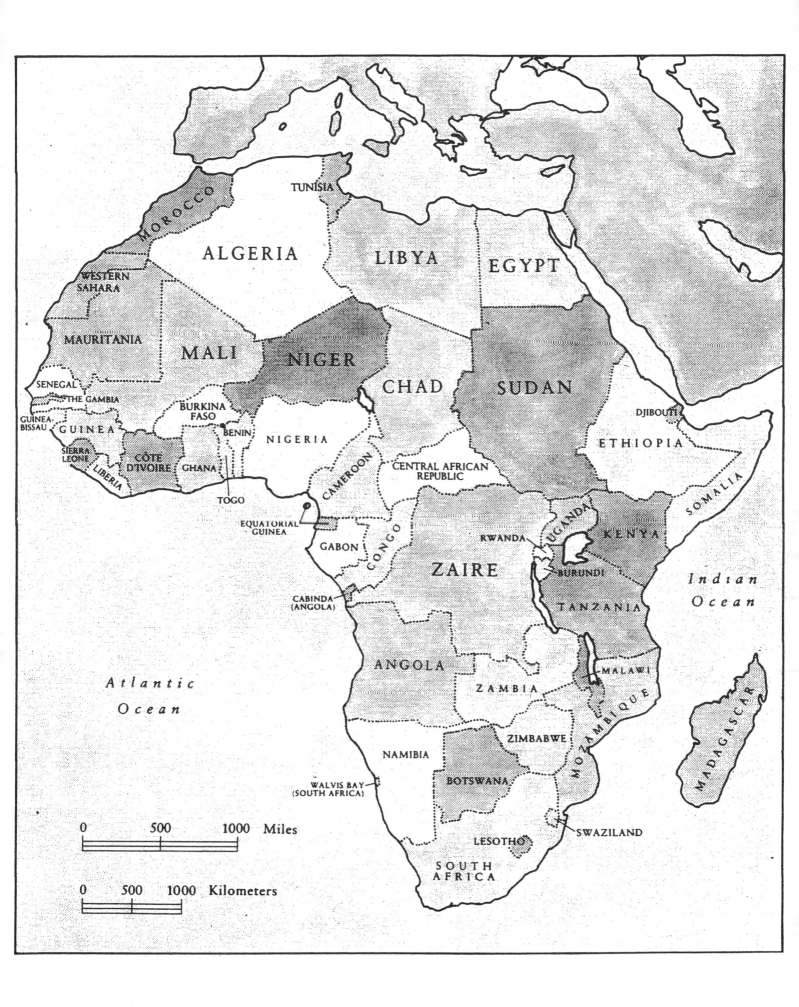

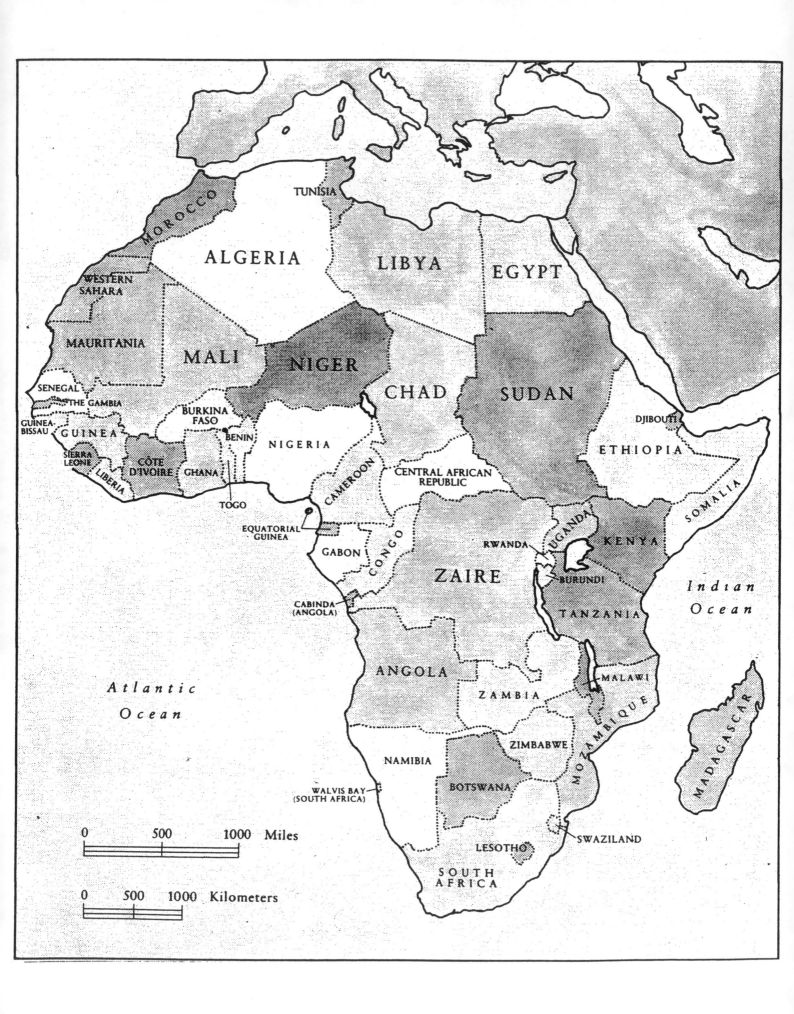

Did You Know That ...

Did you know that Africa is not a country? It's a continent. There are 52 countries in Africa. Africa has more gold, jewels, plutonium, platinum, chrome, and copper than any other continent. Africa's Nile River is the longest river in the world. The Sahara Desert is the largest desert in the world. It is bigger than the entire United States.

Did you know that Africa is more than three times the size of the United States? Did you know that more than 600 million (600,000,000) people live in Africa, over 100 million in Nigeria alone? Human life began in Africa, and people lived there over 4 million years (4,000,000,) before we lived anywhere else. The first civilization and the first city were built in Africa. Did you know that the pyramids of Egypt are the only "Wonders of the World" that still exist?

Did you know that Mount Kilimanjaro in Tanzania is so tall that even though it lies on the equator, its top is covered with snow all year round? The southern part of Africa is so far south that the climate is not tropical but temperate. It snows in South Africa in the summer, yes, the summer, because South Africa is in the Southern Temperate Zone, and so its seasons are the reverse of ours here in the Northern Temperate Zone.

Did you know that South Africa and Southern Africa are not the same? South Africa is one of the many countries in the southern portion of the continent of Africa. Zimbabwe, Zambia, Angola, Mozambique and Namibia are others. South Africa lies at the southern tip of the African continent.

Did you know that Nigeria with 115 million Black citizens has the largest Black population in the world? Brazil with 40,000,000 Blacks has the second largest. The United States with 35,000,000 has the third! *Did you know that?*

Africa Needs Us & We Need Africa

Are you an African? Everyone in the United States came here from somewhere else except the Native Americans (Indians).Whites came from England, Germany, Ireland, Italy and the other nations of Europe. Orientals came from China, Korea, Japan, the Philippines and the other nations in Asia. Blacks came from Africa.

If Italian Americans or Irish Americans or Korean Americans or Chinese Americans want to find out about the "Old Country", their place of origin, they can usually ask their parents or their grandparents to tell them what they remember of the "Old Country", or what they remember their parents and grandparents had told them about it.

We cannot do this. Our parents and grandparents have no direct knowledge of Africa, or knowledge of Africa that has been handed down to them. Why? During slavery Africans were stripped of their languages, their customs, their cultures, so that it would be difficult for them to fight back. Today, as a result, hardly any of us even knows which particular country in Africa our ancestors came from.

A major source of pride and encouragement for Americans is their place of origin, their particular "Old Country". However, we do not even know which "Old Country" we came from. We only know that our "Old Continent" is Africa and little more. Nearly everything we see on television, or in the movies, about Africa is negative. Since we were stripped of our cultures, we have to turn to books to find out about our past and about how our Old Country is doing today.

Today Africa needs us, and we need Africa.

Today our "Old Country" is suffering from famine, war and disease.

Just as Irish Americans help Ireland, Filipino Americans help the Philippines and Jewish Americans help Israel, we can help Africa.

The richest nation in Africa is South Africa. There Blacks had, until recently, been denied the right to vote, and the minority white regime had waged extremely destructive wars against its neighbors. The Algerian government is at war with its own people, and in nearby Egypt dissent is sharply on the rise. AIDS is affecting **many** in Central and Eastern Africa. In Sudan, Somalia, Rwanda and Liberia war and famine rage. Nigeria, most populous country on the continent by far, is run by generals who jailed the winner of the last election. There is a great need for fresh water in much of the continent.

Many lives are shortened because of the lack of clean water supplies. On the bright side, 51 of the 52 countries in Africa are independent. Many possess large amounts of valuable natural resources. Most of Africa's soil is very fertile. Countries like Kenya, Zimbabwe, the Ivory Coast and Libya are doing very well.

Once again we ask: Are you an African?

Once we called ourselves "colored people". Later we said that we were "Negroes". Now we call ourselves "Black". Are we Africans? Jesse Jackson is urging that we recognize our heritage. He says that just as others call themselves Italian Americans, Irish Americans, Jewish Americans, Greek Americans, Chinese Americans etc., we should recognize that we are "African Americans". However, Jesse Jackson cannot define you. Only you can define you.

Are you an African?

AFRICAN HISTORY

5,000,000 B.C.	Human Life Begins
10,000 B.C.	Rise of Nile Valley Civilizations
3,000 B.C.	The Great Pyramids Are Constructed
1500 B.C. - 330 B.C.	The Kingdom of Kush
600 - 150 B.C.	Carthage
1 A.D.	Birth of Christ
350 - 650	Nubia
400 - 1650	Ghana, Mali, Songhay
712 - 1492	Africans Rule Spain
1898	The Battle of Adowa
1945	Selassie Returns to Ethiopia

The oldest skeletons of human beings found so far are about 5 million years old. They were discovered in Oulduvai Gorge in Tanzania. About 12,000 years ago, settled, agricultural civilization begins in the Nile Valley. The greatest architectural structures on earth are the Great Pyramids at Giza, outside Cairo. They are guarded by the Sphinx, and are over five thousand years old. The Egyptian civilization, which produced them, flourished for three thousand years. Carthage's most famous leader, and the world's greatest military genius was Hannibal. At the Battle of Adowa, Emperor Menelik of Ethiopia preserved Ethiopia's independence by defeating the Italians. At this time the rest of the continent was under European rule. In the 1930s Mussolini invaded Ethiopia. A great war ensued. His forces were defeated by the end of World War II, and Menelik's grandson, the Crown Prince, or "Ras Tafari", returns in triumph.

The Land and the People

Most of the people in Africa are Black. In the North African countries most of the people are Arab or mixed, Arab and Black. In South Africa there are 5,000,000 whites. In each country on the African continent there are small populations of Asians and whites mainly living in the cities.

The western part of the continent, particularly along the coast, is the most heavily populated. As we noted earlier, one-sixth of the entire African population is to be found in the West African nation of Nigeria. Ghana, Senegal, Benin, and the Ivory Coast are some of the other countries in West Africa.

The North African countries all have small populations, except for Egypt, which has 60 million citizens. Egypt, Libya and Algeria, all in North Africa, have large oil deposits. In the North we have the very warm, dry Sahara Desert. The people tend to live mainly in the fertile oases scattered throughout the desert or along the banks of rivers, like the mighty Nile that runs through Egypt and down to the center of the continent.

In the West there is mainly rolling grassland. This is called savannah land. In Central Africa we find the rain forests.Zaire is the largest central African country. The East is very mountainous. There are high peaks and many plateaus, flat high plains. Since the land is so high up, the climate is not as hot as it otherwise would be. Mount Kilimanjaro, Africa's highest peak, is found here in the East in Tanzania.

Kenya has large game preserves. These are very big stretches of land, hundreds of miles long, where wild animals are safe from hunters. Visitors come from all over the world to see the elephants, giraffes, lions, zebras, rare birds and other wonderful creatures living freely in the open. Some of the world's best long distance runners come from the high plains of Kenya.

The South, though not as mountainous, is cool and comfortable thanks to the latitude. Remember, the further north you go the cooler it is in the Northern Hemisphere. However, once you cross the equator and continue to go south, the cooler it becomes. Since they lie in the Southern Hemisphere, much of Mozambique, Angola, South Africa and the other nations of Southern Africa have a sub-tropical climate, much like that found in the American states of Georgia and South Carolina.

West Africa is hotter. The center of the continent is also warm. In the North, in the Sahara, it is also hot but not humid. The desert is hot and very dry. The people who live in the dessert are nomadic, that is they travel from place to place. The camel is very important to them. Camels can go for long periods without water. They store water inside themselves in the humps on their backs. Despite the heat, the people who live in the Sahara wear long, flowing robes. These garments actually help keep them cool by trapping the air and causing it to swirl around them as they move.

While many of the people in Africa are rural and are involved with farming, a great deal live in very modern coastal cities such as Mombassa, Cairo, Dakar and Tangiers.

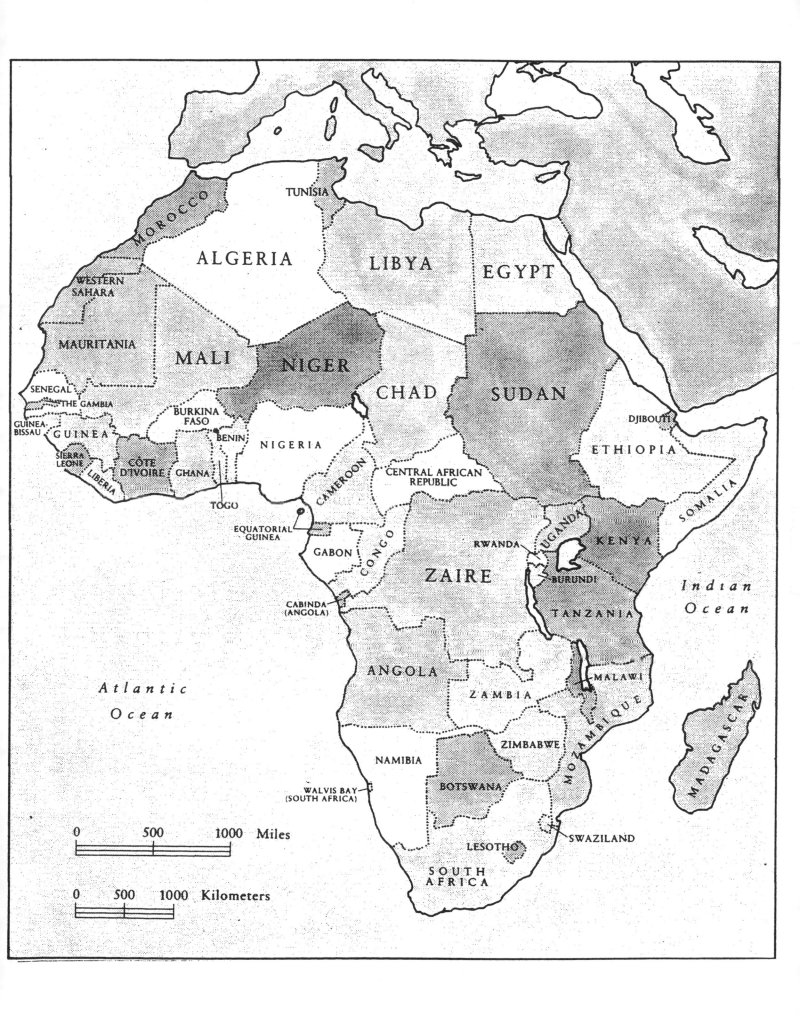

NATION	CAPITAL	AREA	POPULATION
		sq. mile	
Algeria	Algiers	920,000	28,400,000
Angola	Luanda	480,000	11,500,000
Benin	Porto Novo	40,000	5,400,0001
Botswana	Gaborone	230,000	1,500,000
Burkina Faso	Ouagadougou	110,000	10,400,000
Burundi	Bujumbura	11,000	6,400,000
Cameroon	Yaounde	183,000	13,500,000
Cape Verde	Praia	1,600	400,000
Central Afr. Repub.	Bangui	240,000	3,200,000
Chad	N'djamena	500,000	6,400,000
Comoros	Moroni	800	500,000
Congo	Brazzaville	130,000	2,500,000
Cote D'Ivoire	Abidjan	125,000	14,300,000
Djibouti	Djibouti	8,000	600,000
Egypt	Cairo	87,000	62,000,000
Equatorial Guinea	Malabo	10,000	400,000
Eritrea	Asmara	46,000	3,500,000
Ethiopia	Addis Ababa	470,000	56,000,000
Gabon	Libreville	100,000	1,300,000
Gambia	Banjul	4,000	1,100,000
Ghana	Accra	92,000	17,500,000
Guinea	Conakry	95,000	6,500,000
Guinea-Bissau	Bissau	14,000	1,100,000
Kenya	Nairobi	225,000	28,300,000
Lesotho	Maseru	11,000	2,100,000
Liberia	Monrovia	43,000	3,000,000
Libya	Tripoli	680,000	5,200,000

NATION	CAPITAL	AREA	POPULATION
Madagascar	Antananarivo	11,150,000	14,800,000
Malawi	Lilongue	46,000	9,700,000
Mali	Bamako	480,000	9,400,000
Mauritania	Nouakchott	400,000	2,300,000
Mauritius	Port Louis	800	1,100,000
Morocco	Rabat	172,000	29,200,000
Mozambique	Maputo	310,000	17,400,000
Namibia	Windhoek	320,000	1,500,000
Niger	Niamey	490,000	9,200,000
Nigeria	Abuja	360,000	101,200,000
Rwanda	Kigali	10,000	7,800,000
Sao Tome & Principe	Sao Tome	370	100,000
Senegal	Dakar	76,000	8,300,000
Seychelles	Victoria	170	100,000
Sierra Leone	Freetown	28,000	4,500,000
Somalia	Mogadishu	246,000	9,300,000
South Africa	Pretoria	470,000	43,500,000
Sudan	Khartoum	967,000	28,100,000
Swaziland	Mbane	6,700	1,000,000
Tanzania	Dar-es-Salaam	365,000	28,500,000
Togo	Lome	22,000	4,400,000
Tunisia	Tunis	63,000	8,900,000
Uganda	Kampala	91,000	21,300,000
Zaire	Kinshasa	906,000	44,100,000
Zambia	Lusaka	291,000	9,100,000
Zimbabwe	Harare	151,000	11,300,000

In the Beginning

Scientists tell us that the first men and women on earth lived in Africa over 4 million (4,000,000) years ago. The oldest skeletons of human beings have been uncovered by archaelogists in Tanzania. The first civilizations and the first cities were also found in Africa.

Many believe that Plato, Aristotle and the other ancient Greek philosophers were the source of the science and knowledge that we use today. This is not true. Each of these men spent long years studying in Africa in the country called Egypt. This is, perhaps, the most important fact contained in this book. For all the details of how, when, why and where in ancient Egypt that the Greek philosophers studied, with evidence, please see Professor G.M. James', Stolen Legacy.

Imhotep was an Egyptian. He lived thousands of years before Plato and Aristotle. He discovered many scientific principles and is the real "Father of Medicine". The Egyptians were extremely advanced in the study of geometry, astronomy, chemistry, medicine and other sciences. They built the pyramids 4,000 years before Christ was born and 3000 years before Greek civilization began.

People came from all over the world to study in the Egyptian universities and marvel at the wonderful knowledge they had discovered and the mighty pyramids, temples and buildings they had constructed. There were many important African civilizations before and after ancient Egypt.

The people of the Nubian civilization, located in what is today the country of Sudan, established Egypt. They sent some of their people north to the delta of the Nile river, the point at which it empties into the Mediterranean Sea.

They cleaned out the marshes in the Nile Delta and established Egypt's cities. There was always trade and communication between the Egyptians and their Nubian cousins. Whenever Egypt was threatened or invaded, Egypt would turn to Nubia for help. After the Egyptian civilization was overrun by foreigners 666 years before the birth of Christ (666 B.C.), important African civilizations remained and flourished in Ethiopia and Southern Africa. There were also mighty empires in Western Africa particularly the Songhay, Mali and Ghana kingdoms up until 1500 years after Christ (1500 AD).

Africans invaded Spain in the eighth century. They ruled it until 1492, the year that Columbus set sail for the New World.

Population

Nigeria	101,200,000	Guinea	6,500,000
Egypt	62,000,000	Chad	6,400,000
Ethiopia	56,000,000	Burundi	6,400,000
Zaire	44,100,000	Benin	5,400,000
South Africa	43,500,000	Libya	5,200,000
Morocco	29,200,000	Sierra Leone	4,500,000
Tanzania	28,500,000	Togo	4,400,000
Algeria	28,400,000	Eritrea	3,500,000
Sudan	28,100,000	Central Afr. Repub	3,200,000
Kenya	28,300,000	Liberia	3,000,000
Uganda	21,300,000	Congo	2,500,000
Ghana	17,500,000	Mauritania	2,300,000
Mozambique	17,400,000	Lesotho	2,100,000
Madagascar	14,800,000	Namibia	1,500,000
Cote D'Ivoire	14,300,000	Botswana	1,500,000
Cameroon	13,500,000	Gabon	1,300,000
Angola	11,500,000	Gambia	1,100,000
Zimbabwe	11,300,000	Guinea-Bissau	1,100,000
Burkina Faso	10,400,000	Mauritius	1,100,000
Malawi	9,700,000	Swaziland	1,000,000
Mali	9,400,000	Djibouti	600,000
Somalia	9,300,000	Comoros	500,000
Niger	9,200,000	Cape Verde	400,000
Zambia	9,100,000	Equatorial Guinea	400,000
Tunisia	8,900,000	Sao Tome & Principe	100,000
Senegal	8,300,000	Seychelles	100,000
Rwanda	7,800,000		

The African Diaspora

Beginning in the fifteenth century Europe began to exert more and more power over Africa. Africans were being taken as slaves to the New World. By the 19th century, the European countries had carved up all of the African continent, except Ethiopia, into colonies. How did this happen?

One reason why the West African kingdoms fell is that the Sahara desert began to expand southward. Another is that the West African kingdoms fought many wars with each other. One of the main reasons for this warfare was the slave trade.

Europe began trading with Africa in the fifteenth century. They exchanged guns, textiles and rum for slaves. Slaves were obtained by the African kings in war. They were captives, prisoners, taken in war. As the slave trade grew, many wars were fought simply to obtain captives for trade. The destruction caused by these conflicts, and the loss of so many citizens taken away as slaves, badly weakened the societies of Africa.

Nobody knows how many men, women and children were taken as slaves from Africa. It was at least 20,000,000 (20 million). The slave trade lasted from about 1450-1850, 400 years. Some of the slaves were taken to Europe, particularly Spain and Portugal, but most were taken to the New World. Today there are over 100 million descendants of these slaves in the New World, that is, North America, South America, Central America and the Caribbean. This spreading, or dispersing of Africans and their descendants is called the African Diaspora.

Our ancestors were taken from all over the African continent, but especially from West Africa and Angola. They were gathered at points along the

Western coast to be shipped across the Atlantic Ocean. One of the principal points for shipment was Goree Island off the coast of Senegal.

Today the descendants of the enslaved Africans, from throughout the African Diaspora, can come and visit Goree Island as tourists. There they can see the buildings and courtyards in which the enslaved Africans were packed in extremely crowded conditions as they waited to be shipped to the New World. You can touch the chains that hang from the cold stone walls. You can pass through the terrible "Doorway of No Return", the passageway through which our ancestors were taken never to see Africa again. Many say that they can feel the presence of the ancestors. Many break down and cry.

Visitors to Goree Island often stop off in Gambia, the tiny country surrounded on three sides by the nation of Senegal. There they visit the village of Juffure, the home of Kunta Kinte. Alex Haley traced his roots back to a man called Kunta Kinte, from the village of Juffure, in Gambia in his book *Roots*. Each year thousands of African Americans travel to Goree island, and from there go on to Juffure where they can meet the cousins of Alex Haley. Most of the Black population living in America can trace its roots to Gambia, Senegal, Nigeria and the other countries of West Africa. Here is the breakdown of the origins of the slaves shipped to North America during the slave trade.

Nigeria	24%
Angola	24%
Ghana	16%
Senegal/Gambia	13%
Guinea-Bissau	11%
Sierra Leone	6%
Other	6%
Total	100%

Year of Independence

1847	Liberia		
1951	Egypt		
1956	Sudan	Tunisia	Morocco
1957	Ghana		
1958	Guinea		
1960	Chad	Mali	Togo	Congo
	Benin	Niger	Zaire	Gabon
	Nigeria	Senegal	Somalia	Cameroon
	Ivory Coast	Burkina Faso		
	Madagascar	Mauritania		
	Cent. Afri. Repub			

1961	Sierra Leone		
1962	Burundi	Rwanda	Uganda
1963	Kenya	Tanzania	
1964	Malawi	Zambia	
1965	Gambia		
1966	Botswana	Lesotho	
1968	Equatorial Guinea	Mauritius	Swaziland
1969	Guinea-Bissau	Libya	
1975	Angola	Comoros	Mozambique
	Sao Tome		
1976	Seychelles		
1977	Djibouti		
1980	Zimbabwe		
1990	Namibia		

The African's Fight for Freedom

Soon after the slave trade became illegal, in the early 1800s, the nations of Europe began to move from their forts and trading posts along the coast into the heart of the African continent. By the end of the century they had divided up all of Africa, except Ethiopia, into colonies and areas under their indirect control. The Berlin Conference of 1895 drew up distinct boundary lines for each European nation's colonies. It stopped the fighting, but only for a time.

Rivalry amongst the European nations for colonies in Africa led to the First World War (1914-1918) and the Second World War (1939-1945). One-by-one, in the years following the last world war, the nations of Africa gained their independence from the shattered nations of Europe. In some cases, as in Algeria, where France fought a bloody war before surrendering control, the Africans paid dearly for their freedom. Usually, though, the European nations left without much of a fight. Kwame Nkrumah led the African nation of Ghana to independence in 1957. Jomo Kenyatta was another famous African liberation leader. After sharp fighting had taken place in that East African nation, he led Kenya to independence in 1958. In nearby Tanzania, Julius Nyrere became the "Father of the Nation".

During the colonial period, the size of a colony depended on the area of Africa a particular European country had conquered. Once the Africans gained their freedom, the former colony now became an independent nation. However, each of the former colonies contained a number of different African ethnic groups. Most of the fighting that has taken place in Africa, since independence, has been over ethnic issues. A major challenge facing Africa, has been how to end the conflict between identifying with one's modern nation and identifying with one's traditional ethnic group. Usually the largest ethnic group in a nation controls the government. They often use the nation's resources for their own, and neglect the needs of the smaller groups. These smaller ethnic groups sometimes attempt to secede, that is, leave and form their own nation, or join a neighboring nation in which their group is in the majority.

Leaders like Kwame Nkrumah of Ghana in the past and Julius Nyrere of Tanzania and Kenneth Kaunda today, have dealt with this problem by stressing neither identification with the ethnic group nor the nation, but with something much larger, the continent itself. They portray themselves as "Africans" above all else. They strive to unite the entire continent as one. They hope to one day form a "United States of Africa". The idea of looking at all of the continent as one is called Pan-Africanism. The prefix "Pan" means all. Therefore, Pan-Africanism means seeing all of Africa as one. Marcus Garvey firmly believed in Pan-Africanism. Africans living in the New World, when we look toward Africa, we have no choice but to see the continent as a whole, since we do not know our original, individual African ethnic groups. This is just as well, since the conflict between ethnicity and nationality is proving to be so troublesome for Africans in the Motherland.

Independence Days

January
1 Cameroon Sudan
2 Libya

February
18 Gambia

March
2 Morocco
6 Ghana
12 Mauritius
20 Tunisia

April
27 Sierra Leone

May
18 Zimbabwe
27 Togo

June
20 Mali Senegal
25 Mozambique
26 Somalia Madagascar
27 Djibouti
29 Seychelles
30 Zaire

July
1 Rwanda
5 Cape Verde
6 Comoros Malawi
12 Sao Tome & Principe
26 Liberia

August
1 Benin
3 Niger
5 Burkina Faso
7 Ivory Coast
11 Chad
13 Central African Republic
15 Congo
17 Gabon

September
6 Swaziland
10 Guinea-Bissau

October
1 Nigeria
4 Lesotho
9 Uganda
12 Equatorial Guinea
24 Zambia

November
11 Angola
28 Mauritania

December
10 Tanzania
12 Kenya

Mark these dates on your calendar. Does one fall on your birthday? Remember it. Is today an independence day for an African country? When is the next Independence Day? Which country is it?

Nation	Leader	Rule
Morocco	King Hassan II	35 years
Zaire	Pres. Mobutu Sese Seko	31
Gabon	Pres. Omar Bongo	29
Libya	Col. Muammar el-Qaddafi	27
Togo	Pres. Gen. Gnassingbe Eyadema	19
Seychelles	Pres. France-Albert Rene	19
Djibouti	Pres. Hassan Gouled Aptidon	19
Kenya	Pres. Daniel arap Moi	18
Ghana	Pres. Jerry John Rawlings	17
Equatorial Guinea	Pres. Col. Teodoro Obiang	17
Angola	Pres. Jose Eduardo dos Santos	17
Guinea-Bissau	Pres. Joao Bernardo Vieira	16
Botswana	Pres. Quett K.J. Masire	16
Egypt	Pres. Hosni Mubarak	15
Senegal	Pres. Adou Diouf	15
Guinea	Pres. Brig. Gen. Lansane Conte	13
Mauritania	Pres. Maaouye Ahmed Taya	12
Tanzania	Pres. Ali Hasan Mwinyi	11
Swaziland	King Mswati III	10
Mozambique	Pres. Joaquim Chissano	10
Uganda	Pres. Yoweri Mouseveni	10
Central African Repub	General Andre Kolingba	10
Tunisia	Pres. Zine El Abidine	9
Zimbabwe	Pres. Robert Mugabe	9
Sudan	PM Gen. Omar Ahmed Bashir	7
Comoros	Pres. Said Mohammed Djohar	7

Nation	Leader	Rule
Lesotho	King Letsie	6 years
Namibia	Pres. Sam Nujoma	6
Benin	Pres. Nicephore Soglo	5
Burkina Faso	Pres. Blaise Compaore	5
Cape Verde	Premier Carlos Wahon Viega	5
Ethiopia	Pres. Meles Zenawi	5
Sao Tome & Principe	Pres. Miguel Trovoada	5
Zambia	Pres. Frederick T.J. Chiluba	5
Cameroon	Pres. Paul Biya	4
Congo	Pres. Prof. Pascal Lissouba	4
Mauritius	Pres. Cassam Uteem	4
Sierra Leone	Pres. Capt. Valentine Strasser	4
Cote D'Ivoire	Pres. Henri Konam Bedie	3
Eritrea	Pres. Isaias Afwerki	3
Madagascar	Pres. Albert Zafy	3
Niger	Pres. Mahamane Ousmane	3
Nigeria	Gen. Sani Abacha	3
Algeria	Pres. Liamine Zeroual	2
Burundi	Pres. S. Ntibantunganya	2
Gambia	Capt. Yahya Ajj Jammeh	2
Liberia	Pres. David Kpormakpor	2
Malawi	Pres. Bakili Muluzi	2
Rwanda	Pres. Faustin Twagiramungu	2
South Africa	Pres. Nelson Mandela	2
Chad	Pres. Gen. Idriss Deby	1

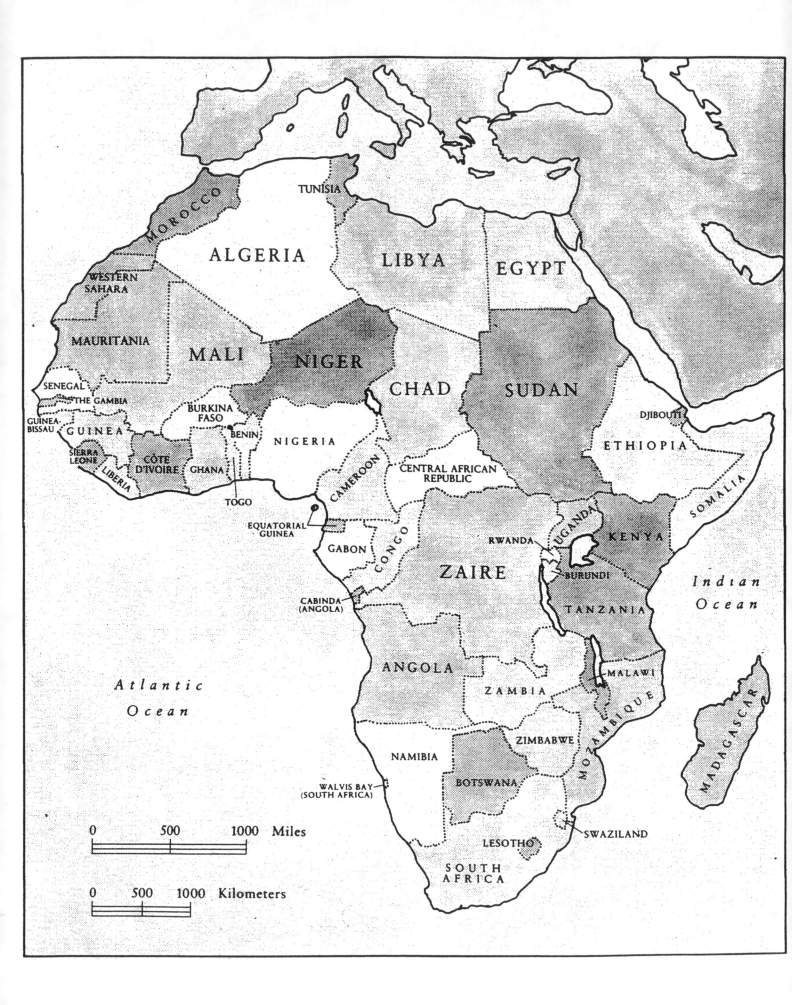

The Wars in Southern Africa

In 1898 Emperor Menelik II of Ethiopia soundly defeated the Italians at the Battle of Adowa. This was the greatest victory of Africans over Europeans since Hannibal's triumph over Rome, two hundred years before the birth of Christ. Just as important to the history of Africa, and Africans, was the tremendous defeat suffered by the South African army in March, 1988 at Cuenevale, Angola. There a combined force of Angolans, Cubans and Namibian freedom fighters routed South Africa's finest soldiers and drove them out of Angola.

After this victory, increasing numbers of white South African young men began to flee the country for fear that they would be drafted. Others openly burned their draft cards. South Africa soon agreed to pull her forces out of Namibia, a country she had illegally occupied for many years. Once she left Namibia, the small white settler population of that country could not hold onto power, and Namibia became independent in January, 1990. In the past, Angola, Mozambique, Zimbabwe and Namibia had served as a buffer zone for South Africa.

The minority white governments in these countries, and their armies, had shielded South Africa from direct attack. South Africa, in return, had given them money and weapons. However, once they fell (Angola and Mozambique in 1975, Zimbabwe in 1979 and Namibia in 1990), South Africa found that three of the countries directly to the north were aiding the freedom fighters fighting for the liberation of South Africa.

Angola, Mozambique, and Zimbabwe, along with Tanzania and Zambia, are referred to as the "frontline states". They earned this name because they are in the frontlines of the battle to end apartheid, and minority white rule in South Africa. Being in the frontlines, they have had to pay a very great price. All have suffered bombing attacks and commando raids. Angola and Mozambique have also been invaded by the South African army. The South Africans have given money and weapons to people in these countries to try and topple their own governments.

Angola and Mozambique have been free for 15 years, but they have had to wage war against South Africa for all of that time. South African soldiers, agents and weapons have killed or crippled over 500,000 people in these two lands since 1975. It is a very common sight to see someone missing an arm or a leg in Mozambique.

Now that South African troops have been driven from Angola, and South Africa has been forced to give up her hold on Namibia, the situation in Southern Africa has changed dramatically. Five years ago, when they first began to see that their days were numbered, the South African government told Mandela they would let him out of prison, if he would tell his followers to stop fighting. Mandela refused, and was kept locked away in jail. In 1990, though, after their terrific defeat in Angola, the continuing economic sanctions, and the mounting internal struggle against apartheid, the South African government let Mandela go without a pledge to give up the armed struggle. Afterwards, they asked him if he would sit down with them to negotiate a settlement.

South Africa

Thousands crowded around the gate to the prison compound. Millions around the world watched the scene on tv, waiting to see the man no one had seen for 27 years, waiting to see Nelson Mandela appear. Everyone had two questions. What would he look like? Will he be able to end apartheid?

Under the system called apartheid, the 35,000,000 Blacks and the 5,000,000 whites in South Africa were kept completely apart. They lived in separate areas. Ate in separate restaurants. Sat in separate parts of the bus, and went to different schools. The two races were totally segregated. The separation of the races in America was called "Jim Crow". Here it was called apartheid.

During World War II many South Africans were supporters of Adolf Hitler and Nazis Germany. Today there is still a large white supremacist political party in South Africa, with ideas like those of the Nazis and the Ku Klux Klan.

The white South African rulers had placed most of the Blacks in small, barrren areas of the country called bantustans. Those allowed to work in the cities, were not permitted to live in the cities. They were forced to travel many miles to separate, crowded Black towns. Soweto, outside of Johannesburg, is the largest of these badly overcrowded Black towns. White workers doing the same jobs as Blacks, would earn up to four times more. Black miners in South

Africa were not allowed to bring their families to live with them. If they were not married, they were forbidden by law from marrying women in the Black towns.

Black children were given inferior education in South Africa. Most died of malnutrition, or disease, before they reached five years of age. In South Africa, Blacks were not allowed to vote. They were not permitted to gather for political protests, meetings or rallies. Thousands were killed for defying these unjust regulations.

People all across the world demanded that the South African government end apartheid, provide equal pay, education and health care for Black and white citizens alike, and extend the right to vote to the vast Black majority. Every country in the world refused to let their athletes compete against South African teams.

Many nations, at the urging of the African National Congress (ANC), instituted economic sanctions, that is, they restricted trade and business with South Africa. The ANC was set up in the 1920s to protest the unfair treatment of Blacks and Asians in South Africa. Many of the early members of the ANC were also members of Marcus Garvey's Universal Negro Improvement Association (UNIA).

Nelson Mandela had been the leader of the ANC when he was arrested, and he remained behind bars for 27 years. On that brisk February day in 1990 when finally he emerged, millions around the world cheered at first sight of the tall handsome man. He was smiling as he walked straight as an arrow holding his wife Winne Mandela's hand. He waved and he looked like a king as he began to lead his people.

In the years since, much has taken place. Mandela negotiated an end to the apartheid laws. He also ran for Prime Minister in 1994 and won. De Klerk, the man he replaced, became one of his two seconds-in-command. However, there was serious violence between different Black groups during the election period, and it continues to flare from time to time. Also, though legal segregation has ended, the social and economic consequences of generations of inequality remain, and the people are impatient for change.

Now that apartheid is over, investments are pouring in from around the world. Many African Americans are participating in this business boom in the richest country on the continent.

Drawing by
Beverly Logan

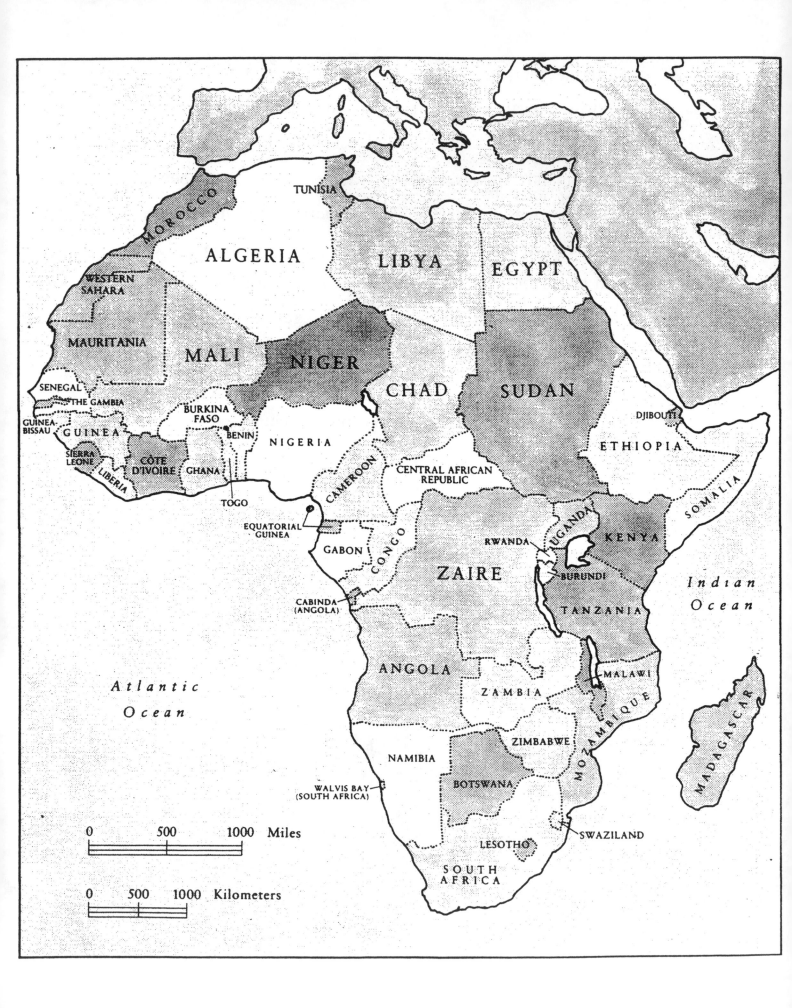

African Liberation Means Our Liberation

At the same time that Martin Luther King was attacking segregation and fighting to win the right for Blacks to vote in the South, Nelson Mandela was doing the same things in South Africa. While King and Malcolm fought to liberate us in this country, Mandela, Nyerere, Kenyatta, Nkrumah and others were fighting to liberate our people in Africa.

By the late 1960s, King and Malcolm both had been killed, while Nyerere (Tanzania), Kenyatta (Kenya) and Nkrumah (Ghana) had won their peoples' liberation, and were leading their nations. Mandela's domain, meanwhile, had become a prison cell, and so it would remain for 27 years. When Mandela was released from jail and came to America, our people saw in him not only the greatest living African leader, but a contemporary of King and Malcolm. (In fact, Malcolm, had he lived, would have been eight years younger than Mandela, King 11 years his junior.) The principal reason that the civil rights movement had not been brutally crushed, like earlier movements to liberate us in this country, was that the United States government was appealing to the newly independent nations of Africa to follow America's leadership, rather than Russia's.

Ever since Reconstruction the American government did little to end lynchings, segregation, or the denial of voting rights in the South. However, when the Civil Rights movement began in 1955 with the Montgomery bus boycott, this government could not afford to let the local officials in the South take matters into their own hands. That would have cost them the support of African nations and other nations of color.

So we see that the fate of our people in this country is intertwined with the fate of our people in Africa. It has always been so. For example, Italy's invasion of

Ethiopia in the 1930s created a storm of protest in Black communities throughout the world. Here in America, as in the Caribbean, funds were raised, and volunteers were recruited to fight the invaders. The attack on Ethiopia increased our awareness of our African heritage and our pride in being of African descent. We should note that Marcus Garvey and W.E.B. DuBois were deeply admired by the African liberation leaders. They read these men's writings very closely, and DuBois, who was still alive at the time, gave very important advice and counsel to Nkrumah, Kenyatta, Nyrere and other African liberation leaders. In turn, they have served to inspire us in our struggle.

Americans of all races and religions have worked together to end apartheid in South Africa. Black political leaders and community groups have played a central role in that effort. Black members of Congress, and other Black leaders and organizations, brought strong pressure on the American government to begin economic sanctions against South Africa and keep them in place. They were also very active in the struggle to release Nelson Mandela from prison and make the African National Congress (ANC) a legal organization in South Africa.

Jesse Jackson worked very diligently in all these efforts, and is very much responsible for bringing the problem of South Africa to the attention of the American people. He spoke at great length about the situation in South Africa in his campaigns for the presidency. It is interesting to note that the great respect and honor shown Nelson Mandela during his visit to this country, makes it much easier for the larger American society to picture a Black man or woman as president of this country.

So we see that every step taken towards the complete and total liberation of the continent of Africa, brings us closer to our total and complete liberation in this country. African liberation is our liberation.

Mickey Leland

In August, 1989 Texas Congressman Mickey Leland and 12 companions crashed into a hillside in Ethiopia in a driving rainstorm. Leland was on his way to visit a relief camp on the border of Ethiopia and Sudan. He had heard that the refugees there were encountering difficulties receiving food supplies. He had insisted on personally investigating the problem. He never reached his destination. He was only 44 years old when he died. He had represented his district in Houston for 11 years. At the time his wife was expecting their second child.

Leland was chairman of the Congressional Black Caucus and Chairman of the House Select Committee on Hunger. He argued mightily in the halls of Congress to create the Committee on Hunger in 1985. Through it, he helped raise hundreds of millions to fight hunger in Ethiopia and throughout Africa and the world. He also greatly expanded the food stamp and job training programs for America's poor. Mickey often told how a young Ethiopian girl died of hunger right before his eyes. He would often exclaim, "I can see her face right now! Every day I can see her face!" It was that image that drove him to argue so eloquently for the food that saved hundreds of thousands of lives. It was that haunting image, and his mighty determination, that led him to his final mission of mercy that turned into tragedy. Congressman Mickey Leland died helping the people of Africa.

"Mickey Leland died as he lived on a mission of mercy and hope for victims of poverty, injustice, racism and hunger...Wherever suffering people existed on our planet, Mickey Leland wanted to be there to help." said Edward Kennedy, senator from Massachusetts.

"Commemorations won't wash away the pain of his wife and his family. Why is it that we wait for the memorial day to honor our contributors? In the future, let us pay homage to the people who lead while they're still breathing among us. Let's never again wait until it is too late." said Attallah Shabazz, daughter of Malcolm X.

Powell

Malcolm

chisolm

HERITAGE   HERITAGE

There a people now forgotten
discovered while others were yet barbarians,
the elements of the arts and sciences.
A race of men now rejected
for their Black skin and woolly hair
founded on the study of the laws of nature,
those civil and religious systems which still govern the universe.

(Count C.F. Volney, Ruins of Empire, 1789)

This race of Blacks is the very one
to which we owe our arts, our sciences,
and even the use of the spoken word.

(Count C.F. Volney, Voyages in Syria and Egypt, 1787)

Universal knowledge
runs from the Nile Valley
toward the rest of the world,
in particular toward Greece
which served as an intermediary.
As a result, no thought, no ideology
is foreign to Africa which was the land of their birth.

(Cheikh Anta Diop, The African Origin of Civilization, 1979)

Language and Religon

Each of the nations of Africa has a European language like English, French, or Portugese as its "official" tongue. This is the language in which government business is handled. It is usually the language of the European country which controlled the nation during the colonial period.

Many also have a "national" language, which is usually the language of the largest ethnic group. Some of the principal, most widely spoken, languages in Africa are: Swahili, Lingala, Wolof, Bantu, and Ewe. Ethnic groups with similar tongues are often closely related to each other. There are about four hundred different ethnic groups in Africa. Each has its own traditional language and religion.

African Traditional Religions (ATRs) were practiced before, during and after the colonial period. Many are connected to the ancient faiths of the Egyptians and other inhabitants of the Nile Valley thousands of years ago. Africans played a major role in the development of the Jewish, Christian and Muslim faiths.

Abraham, the father of both the Jews and the Arabs, is said to have visited Egypt, and his descendants are believed to have lived there for hundreds of years. Christ is the main figure in the Christian faith. While much is known about the last three years of his life, almost nothing is known about his early years, particularly the time between his 12th and his 30th birthdays. Many believe that, like the Greek philosophers, he spent this time studying in Egypt. Up until the time of the artist Michaelangelo, in the 16th century, Christ and his mother were usually shown in sculptures and paintings as being Black. St. Augustine, the man who did much to establish the Christian Church, was an African.

Muhammad, the prophet, used the teachings of Abraham, Moses and Christ, and knowledge revealed only to him, to establish the Muslim faith. He was born six centuries after Jesus on the Arabian peninsula, the huge block of land that lies across the narrow Red Sea on the Northeastern side of the African continent. Many of the people from Arabia were, and are, Black. Muhammad's second-in-command, Bilal, was definitely a Black man. The Muslim faith spread throughout the Middle East and much of Africa. In the eighth century, African Muslims conquered Spain and ruled her until 1492, the year Columbus set sail for the New World.

Ethiopia, the only country in Africa never to have been completely conquered by Europe, has had an important role in several religions. The last Emperor of Ethiopia, Hailie Selassie, is the central figure in the Rastafarian faith. One of the oldest branches of the Jewish faith, the Falashas, comes from Ethiopia. The Coptics, one of the oldest branches of the Christian faith, are also based in Ethiopia.

There is evidence that Blacks founded many of the ancient religions of India, China and Southeast Asia. Indus Khamit in his interesting book, *What They Never Told You in History Class* explains this in great detail.

Africa is Still with Us

The people of the West Indies eat some of the same foods, speak some of the same words and have many of the same customs as their cousins in Africa. African Americans also have many African customs. For example, Gospel music, the Blues and Jazz developed from African rhythms and melodies. Rap music is very similar in form to praise-singing, the West African tradition in which a king's followers make up songs praising him for his accomplishments.

In many African American churches the minister speaks in a lively, colorful manner, and the congregation shouts out their agreement. This is the "call and response" method of communication popular throughout the Motherland. Church services in the West Indies often also use call and response. There are many religions in the West Indies, Cuba and Puerto Rico. Some are based on African religions: Santeria, Pocomania and Voodoo, just to name a few. Reggae, calypso, salsa and the other kinds of music from these countries are also based on African music.

In fact, every place enslaved Africans were brought to in the New World, today has a religion, language and music based on African cultural forms. On the next page we present some examples. Keep in mind that on each island there are several kinds of African music and religion, we only provide one example of each.

When we compare the culture of the peoples of the West Indies with the culture of African Americans, we find that the African influence is greater on the islands than it is here. Why is that? In the West Indies the slaves outnumbered the white population ten-to-one. In America the slaves were less than the white population. Since the slaves were so numerous in the West Indies, they were largely left on their own to provide for themselves and live in their own communities. In the United States this rarely happened. Here the slaves were under much tighter control. Therefore, most of their original African culture was lost. However, in the Sea Islands off the coast of South Carolina and Georgia, the enslaved Africans heavily outnumbered the whites, as in the West Indies. As a result African influences there are very strong.

	JAM'CA	TRINIDAD	HAITI	CUBA	U.S.
MUSIC	Reggae	Calypso	Campo	Rhumba	Jazz
RELIGION	Rastafari	Revivalism	Voodoo	Santeria	"Roots"
LANGUAGE	Patois	Patois	Creole	Cuban Spanish	Black English

The Africans of South Carolina

Have you ever heard of the Gullahs of South Carolina and Georgia? They are also called Geechies. The word "Gullah" is short for the "Gola" people from Angola, and "Geechie" refers to the "Gidzi" people from Sierra Leone. Many of the people in the Sea Islands, off the coast of South Carolina and Georgia, originally came from the areas of Africa that are today the nations of Angola and Sierra Leone.

The Sea Islands are patches of land separated from the mainland by marshes and rivers. The Gullah, or Geechie, people and culture are located on the Sea Islands and in the lowland, coastal areas of South Carolina and Georgia. Their largest community is found in and around Charleston, South Carolina.

In the early 17th century many wealthy Europeans came to Charleston from the Bahamas, Bermuda and Barbados. They brought their slaves and set up large rice plantations in the wet and marshy soil of the Sea Islands. The slaves outnumbered them 15-to- one. These Africans were therefore able to maintain and preserve, up until today, very much of their original culture.

The cobblestone streets of downtown Charleston are lined with old-fashioned, brick and wood-frame buildings. There is usually a cool sea breeze whistling through the leaves of the luxurious palmetto trees. Proud Black women dressed in brightly-colored clothes carry large baskets on their heads. In the market they sell their vegetables, fruits, paintings, carvings and "show baskets" to the eager tourists. They speak with an accent that sounds West Indian. Their tongue is a combination of English and African languages including Wolof and Mandingo.

The Sea Island people are very self-sufficient. They take care of nearly all their needs themselves. They sell each other fish and farm goods. Some families are known for "growing" carpenters, others "grow" tailors, some butchers, some ministers, some builders, and so forth. Everyone on a particular Sea Island is usually related, and the residents, especially the older ones, can trace each other's family tree in great detail. Young people have to travel to other islands to find marriage partners who are not related to them.

Children are very well taken care of. If the natural mother and father are unable to care for a child, other relatives gladly will. Many senior citizens on the Sea Islands say that the reason they have lived so long, and kept in such good health, is that they cannot die until all the children entrusted to their care are grown. Many children learn how to make and to use fishing nets by age 3. Boys and girls are also taught basket-making at a very early age. The Gullah's jewelry, pottery, fans and baskets are similar to ones made in West Africa today.

The islanders are keenly aware of the ways of local animals. Their stories about Brer (Brother) Rabbit and his friends, and foes, are re-tellings of Wolof and Hausa folk tales. In Jamaica, the children hear about Brer Anansi, the spider. The same spider is found in Hausa and Twa folk tales.

In all these stories the small, weak animals are somehow able to outsmart the larger, stronger animals trying to capture and devour them. Most cartoons, especially those from years ago, involve small, weak animals being chased and hunted by much larger beasts, just like the tales of Brer Anansi and Brer Rabbit. In fact, the most famous cartoon character is a rabbit. Do you remember his name? Do you think he might have been copied from Brer Rabbit? And what about the other weak, but very smart, animals that are always chased in the cartoons? Have they too been copied from the African folk tales? Which do you think came first, the cartoons or the African folk tales?

African Folk Sayings

When the mouse laughs at the cat there is a hole nearby.
(Nigeria)

. . . .

In a court of fowls the cockroach never wins his case
(Rwanda)

. . . .

What is said over the dead lion's body could not be said
to him alive. (Zimbabwe)

. . . .

Copying everybody else all the time, the monkey one
day cut his throat. (South Africa)

. . . .

African Words in the English Language

Did you know that there are many African words in the English language. For example, okay, yam, jazz, okra, tote and goober. In Wolof the word "hipicat" means someone whose eyes are wide open. The Wolof word "derega" means to understand. Is that where the phrase, "Dig me?" came from?

The Mandingo have an expression, "i golo don m dolo!" It translates as "put your skin in my hand!" Many African names are popular in the United States particularly in the South. Names like "Mingo", "Fanny" and "Reena" are African in origin. Very often African children are named after the day of the week on which they were born.

	MALE	FEMALE
SUNDAY	Kouassi	Akouassiba
MONDAY	Kodio	Adioula
TUESDAY	Kouamina	Aminaba
WEDNESDAY	Kouakau	Akouba
THURSDAY	Yao	Abby
FRIDAY	Kofi	Afouba
SATURDAY	Kouami	Amoriba

Doesn't Kofi sound a lot like Cuffee? Many feel that Kouami resembles Tommy, and that is perhaps why it is so popular. Are there any other names that seem to resemble African day names?

Traces of Africa in America Today

Right outside Mexico City there are some fascinating statues. They are giant stone heads, some nearly 16 feet tall. The faces are African. They are 2300 years old. Columbus, we are told, discovered the New World 500 years ago. However, these giant stone heads indicate that nearly two thousand years before that Africans were here. How did they get here?

Professor Ivan Van Sertima in his famous book, _They Came Before Columbus_, provides an answer. According to Van Sertima, many hundreds of years ago, an Egyptian trading ship sailing off the West African coast was blown out to sea. The currents carried it across the Atlantic Ocean all the way to the New World, to Mexico.

The soldiers and sailors on board, because of their superior strength, weapons and technology, became kings over the Indians. He has detailed evidence to support his ideas. He points to, among other things, the direction of the currents in the Atlantic Ocean, the pyramid-shaped monuments built in ancient Mexico, and extensive archaeological findings in the area. In the Museum of Natural History, in Manhattan, one of these giant stone heads is on display for all the world to see.

However, it is the Brooklyn Museum that has the most impressive artifacts of ancient Africa. It contains hundreds of statues and carvings from ancient Egypt and the Nile Valley. Some are four thousand years old! It is truly wonderful to see, and to touch, the stone faces of African kings and queens from eons ago. No one who encounters them can ever doubt that the Egyptians were an African people, a Black African people. In no way did they resemble the actors Hollywood has selected to play their parts.

Once a year, however, the spirit of Africa comes vividly to life right outside the big brass doors of the Brooklyn Museum. Right there, every year, on the first Monday in September, they erect the reviewing stand for New York City's largest parade, the West Indian Day Parade. The crowd sometimes numbers over two million.

Floats with raging steel bands, playing calypso music, are surrounded by thousands of brightly costumed dancers. Those watching dance along too and eat and drink and meet old friends. Meanwhile, the rollicking calypso tunes come echoing up tree-lined Eastern Parkway one after the other, after the other. The rhythms, the joy, the feeling is truly overwhelming. You cannot believe it unless you see it. Have you ever been to the West Indian Day Parade. If you are in New York next year be sure to come and participate in this joyous colorful celebration of our African heritage.

Food in Africa

West Africans like peppers. They also use a lot of tomatoes and okras. They like stews flavored with meat, seafood, chicken or peanuts. West Africans have many different fruits and vegetables with each meal. Smoked fish cooked in palm oil with green vegetables is a favorite in Gambia.

There are many different kinds of yam in Africa. Some individual yams can weigh up to 20 pounds. Cassava is another important African foodstuff. Cassava, yam or other starches are often boiled, pounded in a mortar with a heavy pestle. This thick dish is called fufu .

Couscous is rice, wheat or millet, or a mixture of all three ground into powder. Traditionally, Africans do not eat much red meat. Their protein mainly comes from nuts, fish, seafood and chicken. Palm wine is a favorite drink.

Meals are, according to custom, eaten with the hands only. Water is always provided to cleanse the fingers before, during and after the meal. A piece of fufu is broken off and this serves as your spoon as you dip into this or that sauce or side dish. Only the right hand is used for eating. Traditionally, men, women and children eat separately. Visitors are always fed. The thoughtful guest leaves a bottle of liquor for the family.

Marriage in Nigeria

Let us visit a wedding ceremony among the Ibo people of Nigeria. Listen to the blessings and the instructions given to the couple by their families.

Family of Bride Says:

"My dear daughter, we bless you and give you all our love. Now that you are leaving us, we hope you will enoy your new home. As you know, a woman takes good care of her husband; you cook for him and help him throughout his distress.

My dear son-in-law, now that you take our daughter, we hope you take good care of her and provide her needs and be a faithful husband to her."

Family of Groom Says:

"Our dear daughter-in-law you will not regret being a part of this family. Happiness is our motto and happy we shall make you. Love is in our home, and love we shall give you. We shall make you happy and pleased to be a part of our family. May you and our son have many children; we await our grandchildren."

Vivian Smith

Playtime in Rural Liberia

A child is a child wherever he lives whatever his cultural background. He laughs and cries, runs, jumps, imitates older people, and tests his strength with his friends. In the large cities, Liberian children can be seen riding tricycles, pulling wagons, playing with mechanical toys, and dolls that walk, talk, and wet. But away from the cities where there is down-to-earth existence, children's toys are more traditional.

In these interior areas a little girl is much more concerned with helping the female members of her large family rather than playing with dolls. A girl who at age 7 or 8 is trusted with carrryig a tiny baby on her back has little or no time for dolls. If she does, her first, and usually her only, doll will be made with a bamboo stick and which she uses to practice braiding, a skill she will always use. Sometimes she carries this stick doll on her back, if she has not already been given a real baby to carry. She helps her mother carry things and helps tend their goods in the market. The market is very busy with buying and selling and tending goods and the swapping of exciting news and bits of gossip.

In place of a wheel toy the tiny boy enjoys his rough home-made "go-so" push toy which he patiently watched his loving father, grandfather, or uncle build just for him. He probably enjoys it more than his city cousins enjoy their numerous fantastic, wheeled toys. He is not about to let any other child take it from him

Nigerian children love ball games. Traditionally their first balls are made of skin, grass, ivory, palm fiber, raffia or wood. In the cities they have balls made of rubber, metal or plastic. In the past the Liberian child developed his athletic skills individually, today, though, team games such as hopscotch and circle games have been introduced and the children love them.

The play period for the children in the more remote areas of Liberia, and other African countries, is not long. Very soon the society reaches out and pulls them in to carry their own small share of the load. When a girl can care for a real live baby, a doll has little chance for lasting importance. A boy who can use his own small cutlass has neither time nor desire for a knife that's only for play.

Jean Mowatt

GO·SO TOY

BAMBOO STICK DOLL

Family Wisdom

What the child says he has heard at home.

The most beautiful fig may contain a worm.

It is a bad child who will not take advice.

Quarrels end, but words once spoken never die.

When you know who his friend is, you know who he is.

Love is like a baby: it needs to be treated tenderly.

If relatives help each other, what evil can hurt them.

The ruin of a nation begins in the homes of its people.

He may say that he loves you. Wait and see what he does for you.

When a woman is hungry she says,
"Roast something for the children that they may eat."

Don't try to make someone hate the person he loves, for he will still go on loving,
but he will hate you.

Three kinds of people die poor: those who divorce, those who incur debts, and
those who move around too much.

If your son laughs when you scold him, you ought to cry, for you have lost him; if he cries, you may laugh, for you have a worthy heir.

Proverbs are of great importance in the Motherland. They are not just wise "sayings". In fact, they are the collected wisdom of the ages condensed into small packets that can be used at appropriate times to solve difficulties. For example, amongst some traditional African ethnic groups, legal questions are solved by an exchange of proverbs. Just as lawyers in the courtroom argue their cases by referring to past cases (precedents), Africans can sometimes solve their difficulties by discussing them in a conversation in which proverbs are used to explain each side and counter the opponent. Proverbs are so important in Africa, that many proverbs are themselves about the importance of proverbs. For example:

Proverbs are the daughters of experience.

A wise man who knows his proverbs can reconcile difficulties.

When the fool is told a proverb its meaning has to be explained to him.

A proverb is the horse of conversation; when the conversation lags, a proverb revives it.

Many African proverbs have been "borrowed" by the English language. For example, the famous saying attributed to Shakespeare, "Familiarity breeds contempt; distance breeds respect." is African in origin. Here are some others. In the parenthesis we place the English variation.

Don't kick a sleeping dog.
(Let sleeping dogs lie.)

Seeing is better than hearing.
(Seeing is believing.)

A half loaf is better than no bread
(A half a loaf is better than none.)

He who receives a gift does not measure.
(Never look a gift horse in the mouth)

The dog's bark is not might, but fright.
(The dog's bark is worse than his bite.)

Let him speak who has seen with his eyes.
(Seeing is believing.)

He who cannot dance will say the drum is bad.
(A good workman never blames his tools.)

It's the calm and silent waters that drown a man.
(Still waters run deep.)

No matter how long the night, the day is sure to come.
(Nights darkest hour comes just before the dawn.)

Were they really "borrowed" from English, or did the English just happen to come up with similar proverbs on their own? We must keep in mind that the wordings may have been changed gradually over time. Also, remember that they are translations from African languages, and so when translating from one tongue to another slight changes are often made because exact translations often loose the rhythm, and pleasing sound of the original. One more thing. During the Middle Ages there was a saying, still in use today, "As far away as Timbuktu!" Timbuktu was the center of learning a thousand years ago, and people travelled from all over Africa, Europe and Asia to come to the great university in this West African city. Is that were the English picked up these proverbs? Here are some more African proverbs.

A roaring lion kills no game.

To try and to fail, is not laziness.

Move your neck according to the music.

One cannot both feast and become rich.

One falsehood spoils a thousand truths.

It is the fool's sheep that break loose twice.

Singing "Halleluia" everywhere does not prove piety.

The horse who arrives early gets good drinking water.

It is better to travel alone than with a bad companion.

As the wound inflames the finger, so thought inflames the mind.

If the palm of the hand itches, it signifies the coming of great luck.

Advise and counsel him; if he does not listen let adversity teach him.

The day on which one starts out is not the time to start one's preparations.

Africa Was Our Home...
Africa Was Our Home...
Africa Was Our Home...

A frica was our home

F ar across the seas.

R e-awakening our forgotten past

I s an almost impossible task.

C an we succeed if we try?

A frica, can we find you?

Can We Find You?...
Can We Find You?...
Can We Find You?...

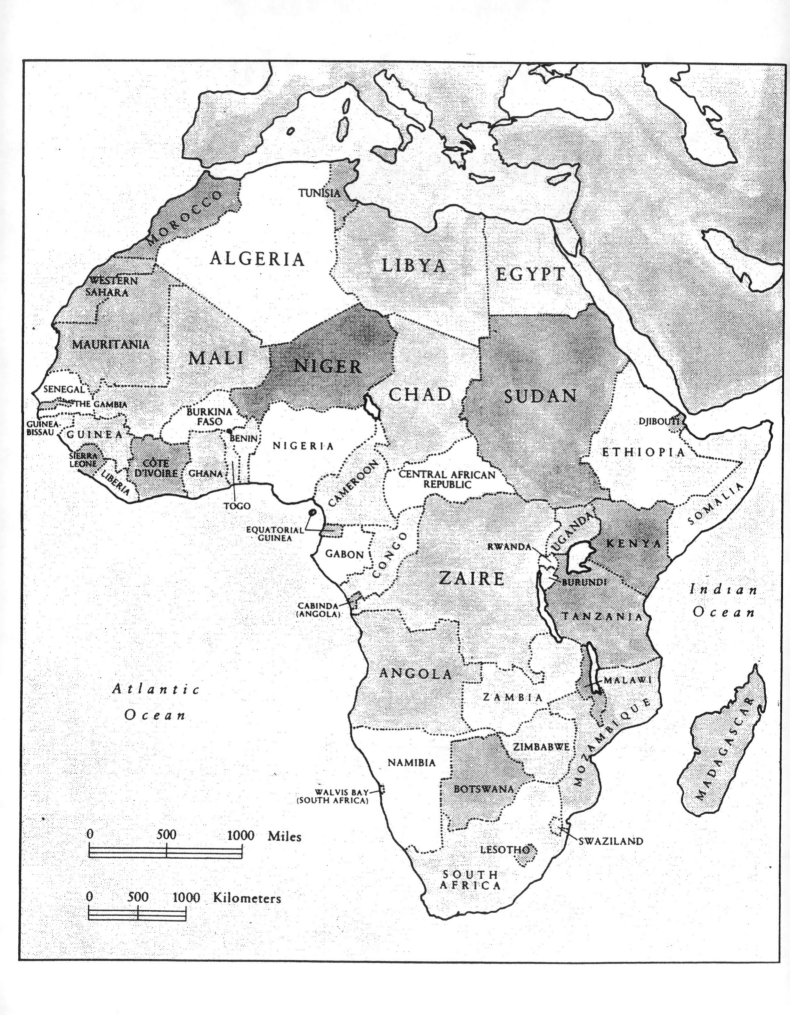

G ambia is the tiny country surrounded by Senegal

A lex Haley traced his Roots to the town of Juffure

M illions have been inspired by this magnificent tale

B y the hope it kindles in all our hearts

I f we search and search and search

A ll of us can find our Roots

S enegalese merchants are found in New York

E agerly they await you with their many wares

N ew Orleans and Charleston were U.S. slaveports

E ighteen Million Africans were shipped through

G oree island located off Senegal's shores

A fter leaving here they'd see their homes no more

L ong ago these our ancestors were wrenched from Africa's shore

G hana was the first African nation to be free

H ow many, many others have followed on that path

A ll save South Africa are now standing on their own

N krumah was her champion, the champion of us all

A frica united was the dream he lived and died for

E gypt was the light of the ancient world

G reat and glorious thinkers were born and reared here

Y ears and years before Plato, Socrates and Aristotle

P yramids rose up from out of the desert sands

T o touch the stars and enlighten our minds

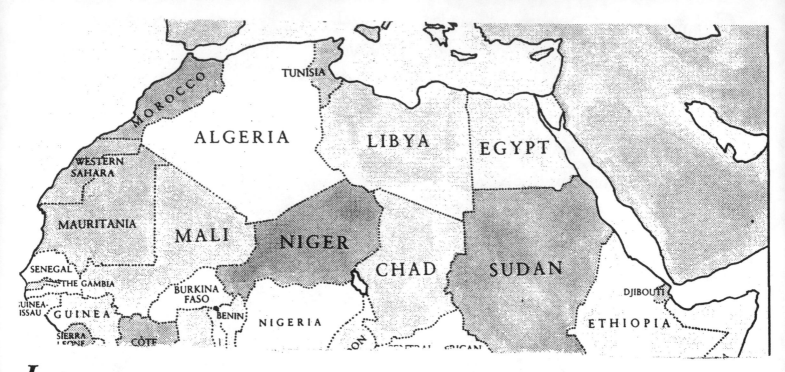

L ibya is a North African country

I t is small in population but rich in oil

B enghazi and Tripoli are the major cities

Y ou'll find Lybia lying along Egypt's western side

A merica has clashed with her many many times

C had lies in the Sahara

H ussein Habre is her leader

A rmies here clash in dessert sands

D rought kills more than the guns

S udan is Africa's largest nation

U nder the dessert sun she stretches

D ivided between Arab and Black

A ll her people must unite as one

N ubia was her ancient name

A lgeria fought a great war to be free

L ibya and Tunisia border her on the east

G ood health care is here provided for all

E ducation levels and literacy rates are high

R evolution cost her a half million people

I nternal problems are returning today

A frica hopes her peace can be maintained

K enya is a beautiful country in East AFrica
E lephants, gazelles and lions graze rolling plains
N o one to disturb them as they go about their lives
Y et she has many towns and mighty cities too
A frica is proud of the balance she maintains

D jibouti is a tiny country
J utting out on the Horn of Africa
I ssas and Afars, her two ethnic groups
B loody wars have raged between the two
O utside nations take sides in the fight
U ntil her peoples learn to live in peace
T hey will prevent their country from developing

M alagasy is a giant island once called Madagascar
A bout 150,000 different plants and animals
L ocated here cannot be found elsewhere
A bout 300 miles, she lies, off Africa's coast
G ood weather blesses this subtropical island
A fricans from the mainland have migrated here
S o much of her forest is being destroyed to make farmland
Y ears from now many of her unique life forms may be gone

U ganda lies in East Africa
G reat mountain plains lay in her interior
A min was once her terribly feared leader
N ow that he is gone peace has not yet come
D eep divisions remain amongst her peoples
A IDS has killed many in this troubled land

E thiopia is a very old land
T he Hebrews are ancient here
H ailie Selassie was her emperor
I mages of Lions and Kings lie in her past
O ld churches here are hewn from stone
P ast glories may yet live again
I f she ends her dessert wars
A nd her peoples dwell in peace

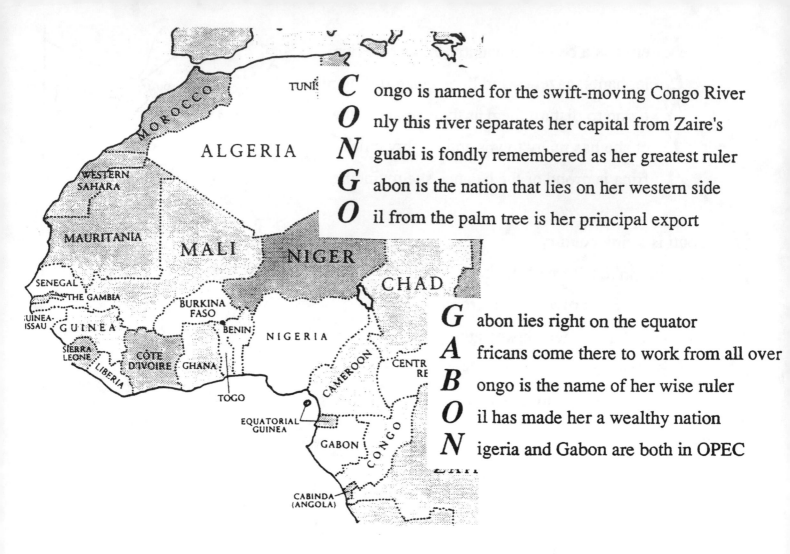

Congo is named for the swift-moving Congo River
Only this river separates her capital from Zaire's
Nguabi is fondly remembered as her greatest ruler
Gabon is the nation that lies on her western side
Oil from the palm tree is her principal export

Gabon lies right on the equator
Africans come there to work from all over
Bongo is the name of her wise ruler
Oil has made her a wealthy nation
Nigeria and Gabon are both in OPEC

Colonized by Britain and France

Aluminum is the primary export

Muslims and Christians are of equal numbers

Exported too are cocoa, coffee, rubber and timber

Republic of Cameroon speaks both French and English

Of all the modern day countries in Africa

Only Cameroon has two official languages

Nigeria is her mighty neighbor to the North

Niger

She is the largest country in West Africa, but it has only 1/15th the population of Nigeria. 97% of the population is Muslim. It is completely landlocked, and is bordered by 7 different countries. Look at the map and see if you can name these 7 countries.

B enin is in West Africa

E veryone once called her Dahomey

N ow she's lost her famous ancient glory

I n chains her people were take to the land called Brazil

N ever again did they see her shores, but their descendants speak her language still

S ierra Leone

I s a former English colony

E stablished to settle freed slaves.

R uled by the ex-slaves descendants for many years,

R ecently the local people rose up and revolted.

A t the present time she enjoys an uneasy peace.

L iberia was also a colony for former slaves.

E ventually she too suffered a terrible revolt.

O nly if the turmoil ceases can these nations grow.

N ow is the time to look ahead with hope and confidence.

E ventually, we pray, their troubled pasts will be forgotten

N igeria is the most populated country in Africa

I bos, Hausas, Yorubas and many others live here

G reat civilizations flourished in her distant past

E thnic strife and before that colonialism laid her low

R ivers and rivers of oil flow beneath this rich, rich land

I f her peoples can bring themselves to forget their disputes

A ll will live in peace and enjoy true and lasting prosperity

S outh Africa is now free.

O nly time will tell us if

U nder the leadership of

T he ANC and Nelson Mandela

H er success shall be complete

A ll Africans look to her

F or leadership and direction

R ich in resources and people and

I nternationally reknowned

C an South Africa end its internal squabbling

A nd become the greatest success story of the Diaspora?

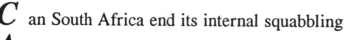

A ngola was Africa's first colony

N eto led the independence movement

G ood news came from here in 1988

O ccupation forces of apartheid were defeated

L oyal troops now control all the precious land

A ngola won with the help of soldiers sent from Cuba

Z imbabwe

I s named for a mighty ancient empire

M onuments and cities of towering stone

B uilt to last forever remind us of this past

A fter 14 years of war it became free in 1979

B ut white settlers remain and work with the government

W ith Zimbabwe's help the freedom fighters of the ANC

E ventually brought apartheid South Africa to its knees

B otswana is a completely landlocked country
O nly through South Africa can she engage in trade
T swana is the nation's principal ethnic group
S ixty Thousand Botswanans work in South Africa
W ithout South Africa the economy would collapse
A million people live in this land the size of Texas
N amibian freedom fighters had been based here
A partheid's end also meant freedom for Botswana

T anzania is ruled wisely
A ll the people share the wealth
N one suffer while others prosper
Z anzibar is the very large island
A lso prieviously known as Madagascar
N ow joined with old "Tanganyika"
I n the proud nation, Tanzania
A ll Africa admires its stability

N amibia,
A ngola's neighbor,
M ay one day become
I ndependent economically
B ecause of its mineral wealth.
I nternally, Namibia is now stable
A fter driving out the armies of apartheid.

M ozambique had seen terrible turmoil
O pposition groups were aided by South Africa
Z ambia and Zimbabwe sent their troops to help
A ngola was under similar South African attack
M achel led Mozambique to victory against the Portugese
B ut seven years after the revolution ended he was slain
I n mid-air the South Africans shot down his plane
Q uite a number of Mozambique's citizens had died
U nder armies sent by the land run by apartheid
E ventually, though, Mozambique shall thrive

DO YOU KNOW THE CAPITAL CITIES?

WRITE THEM IN RED

SEE P. 12

CAN YOU FILL IN THE NAMES?

Countries

```
B   I   D   N   U   R   U   B

S   O   R   O   M   O   C   E

O   H   T   O   S   E   L   N

G   R   I   S   O   R   E   I

O   E   L   O   W   I   M   N

T   G   H   A   N   A   F   G

A   I   B   M   A   Z   N   L

T   N   A   M   I   B   I   A
```

Can you find the names of the African countries that appear below in the puzzle? Circle the ones that you can identify. (The names can appear horizontally, vertically, diagonally, or backwards.)

Lesotho	Burundi	Ghana	Niger
Zaire	Zambia	Namibia	Comoros
Botswana	Benin	Togo	

Languages

```
S  E  W  O  L  O  F  Y
T  W  I  B  O  Z  A  O
A  R  A  B  I  C  L  R
K  O  F  H  A  R  A  U
A  O  E  S  I  O  G  B
N  W  U  G  E  L  N  A
E  A  M  H  A  R  I  C
H  E  D  N  E  M  L  X
```

Below there are 14 of the many languages of Africa. Each of them is hidden in the puzzle above. How many can you find?

Swahili	Hausa	Arabic	Kiro
Yoruba	Lingala	Fon	Ewe
Amharic	Mende	Wolof	Ibo
Twi	Akan		

Afterwards try your best to discover at least one country in Africa where each of these languages is spoken. Talk to your friends, teachers, parents and neighbors. See if they can help you. Can you find any books that would help? Each of these languages is spoken in at least several countries so it is not as hard as it seems.

Leaders

P	S	R	E	I	G	L	A
P	E	T	O	H	M	I	B
L	M	A	C	H	E	L	O
S	Q	A	D	A	F	F	I
H	T	X	N	I	M	A	M
A	V	T	A	D	A	S	O
K	N	Y	E	R	E	R	E
A	B	M	U	M	U	L	S
E	B	A	G	U	M	U	A

Can you identify the African leaders listed below in the puzzle that appears above?

Lumumba	Sadat	Shaka
Amin	Mandela	Imhotep
Nyerere	Qadaffi	Mugabe

Can you match the description with the leader?

1   I am the jailed leader of the African National Congress (ANC)?

2   I am the leader of the nation of Tanzania?

3   I was the famous warrior chief of the Zulus?

4   I led Zaire to independence, and was assassinated in 1960?

5   I am the leader of the nation of Libya?

6   I led Zimbabwe to independence in 1980, and I am her leader today?

7   I was the leader of Egypt assassinated in 1979?

8   I ruled Uganda in the 1970s, but the people drove me out of power?

9   I am the real "Father of Medicine"?

Lumumba	Sadat	Shaka
Amin	Mandela	Imhotep
Nyerere	Qadaffi	Mugabe

How this Book was Written

In the Spring of 1988 I hit on an interesting idea for a term project. I asked each student in two of my Black Studies classes to pick a particular country in Africa and find out everything they could about it. I instructed them to collect articles, consult almanacs, draw up fact sheets, write essays, visit embassies, go to libraries, and to try to locate and interview individuals from the country they had selected. They were asked to keep their findings and writings in a folder, and to turn them in at the end of the term.

I organized the students into five groups, or panels: Northern Africa, Southern Africa, Western Africa, Eastern Africa and Central Africa. Each panel worked closely together locating and preparing their materials. Each was given a day to make a joint presentation sharing their findings with the entire class.

They put heart and soul into their projects, thoroughly researching their countries and regions. The group presentations were not only factual, but creative and very thought-provoking. We all learned from each other as we strove mightily to reconnect ourselves to the Motherland. One day towards the end of the term, I made an offhand remark that maybe some of us could work together over the summer to compile some of the materials into a book for eventual publication. Thus, was born _Africa is Not a Country: It's a Continent!_

We met on Saturdays. Many brought their children with them. We called our little group "Africa Unlimited", and our motto became, "Africa knows no boundaries!" In fact, Africa Unlimited soon spread beyond the original group of volunteers from the two classes, as others heard what we were doing, and asked us to include them.

Despite the fact that many had full-time jobs and families and attended summer school, they still somehow found the time to meet on Saturdays, and visit libraries and embassies and conduct interviews during the week. Their dedication was truly astounding. One of us would always take the children into another room and try to keep them entertained. It would not take long, however, for them to rejoin us interjecting their questions, excitement and enthusiasm.

The goal that Africa Unlimited set for itself was to organize, update and expand our extensive files on Africa, based on the folders of the students. I wrote Africa is Not a Country using the information we compiled and my own prior, and subsequent, research. Africa Unlimited is working on a second, expanded edition of this book, and many other projects. (Would you like to join us? See how in the following pages.)

In addition to the names listed on the title page under Africa Unlimited, the following were the members of the two classes whose folders on each country started the ball rolling. Karen Bernard, Kim Birchwood, Edwin Blount, Aprille Brown, Samuel Burney, Camille Cedeno, Andre Clarke, Wendy Cobb, Maria Cutrone, Rohan Defreitas, Charles Glover, Nardia Somers, Daniel Grayson, Sherry Johnson, Jamie Lepow, Dawn Mabry, Alford McBean, John Morris, Lissette Nieves, Wendy Parker, Wayne Phillip, Lorraine Pierre, Carolie Rigg, Alberto Samuels, Lori Shelton, Liza Skendros, Esmie Smith, Manita Swamipersaud, Lisa Tamplenizza, Yvette Wilkinson, Mark Williams, and Develon Young

Also, Roy Adams, Denise Armour, Andrene Austin, David Banks, Angela Barker, Martha Barnes, Nigel Bedeau, Elliot Bowman, Enbeston Cain, David Elias, Ernest Enoma, Marjorie Giordani, Kolleen Hinckson, Lynn Hopkins, Carol Hunter, Byron Jefferson, Jyoti Kateria, Sangeeta Kataria, Leslie Mathis, Tammi Murray, Richard Romero, Wanda Sanders, Giyora Simantov, Shaleen Soberanis, Shepard Toney, Olga Vasquez, John Vega and Katrice Wheeler.

OURSTORY
1950 - 2000

OURSTORY 1950-2000: A HISTORY OF AFRICAN AMERICA

A fascinating, easy-to-understand, handy guide to the organizations, personalities and events of the last 50 years of Black history in America!

A HISTORY OF AFRICAN AMERICA

DR. ARTHUR LEWIN

CARIBBEAN

WEST INDIAN, AFRICAN-AMERICAN OR AFRICAN?

A PEOPLE'S SEARCH FOR IDENTITY, WEALTH AND POWER!

$11.95

CARIBBEAN

WEST INDIAN AFRICAN-AMERICAN OR AFRICAN?

DR. ARTHUR LEWIN

ORDER FORM

Ourstory 1950-2000...... $12

Africa Is Not A Country..... $12

Caribbean, West Indian, African.... $12

TOTAL

Name _____

Street _____

City _____

Mail to:

Clarendon Publishing Company
Box 125 • Peoples Plaza
100 Ryders Lane
Milltown, NJ 08850